HUMAN BODY ACTIVITY BOOK FOR KIDS

THIS BOOK BELONGS TO

____

Amelia Sealey

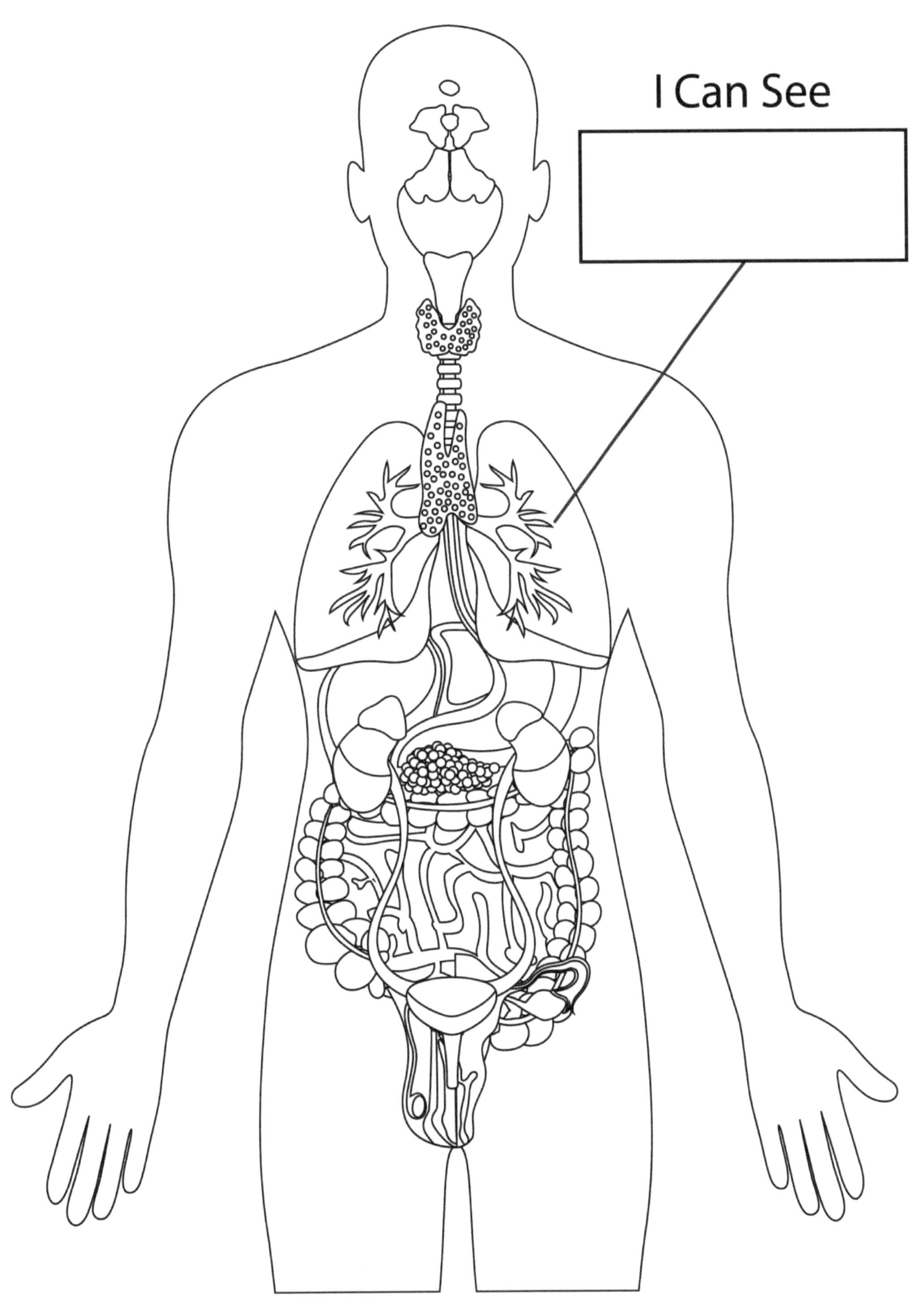

I Can See

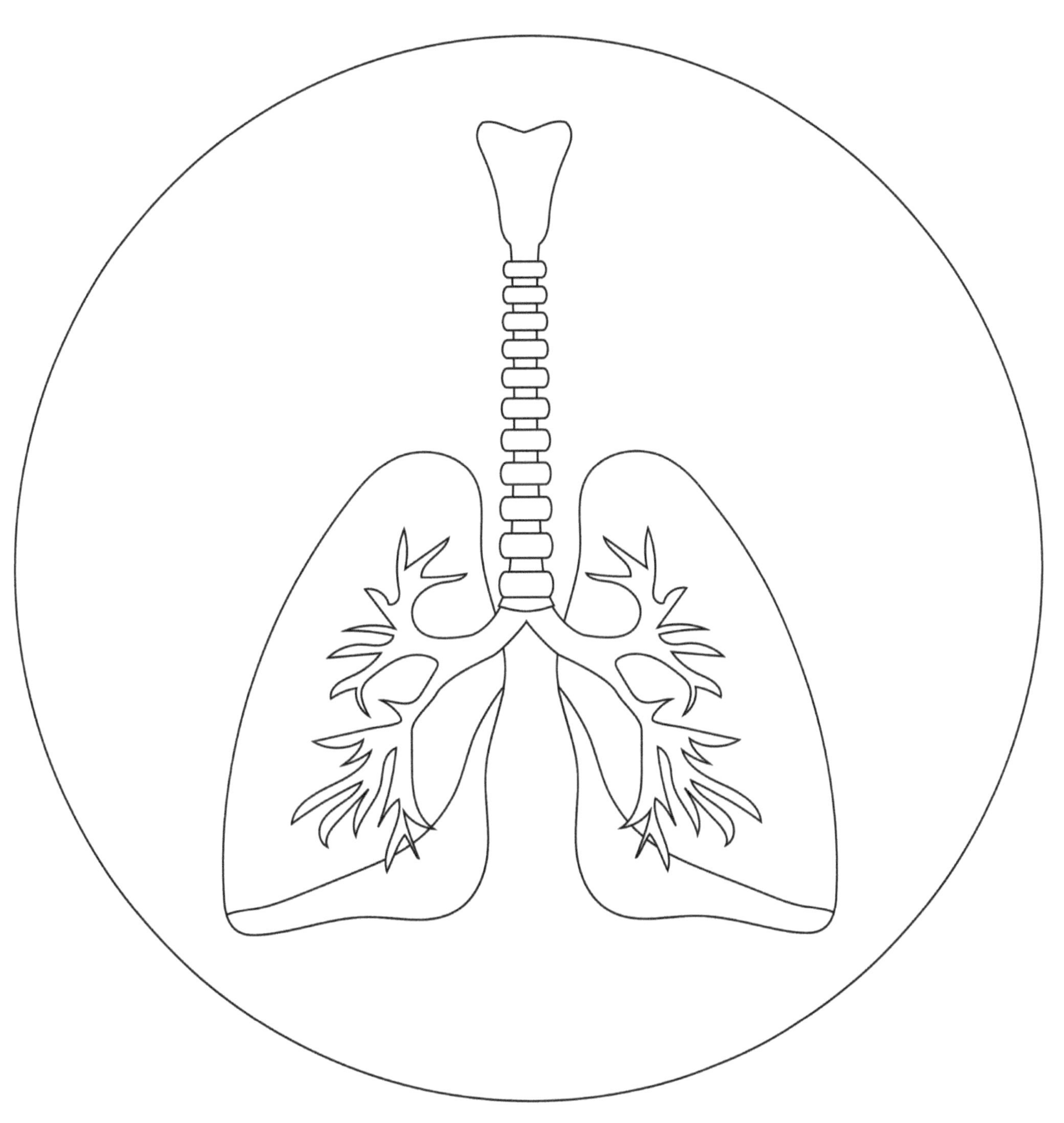

Lungs

I Can See

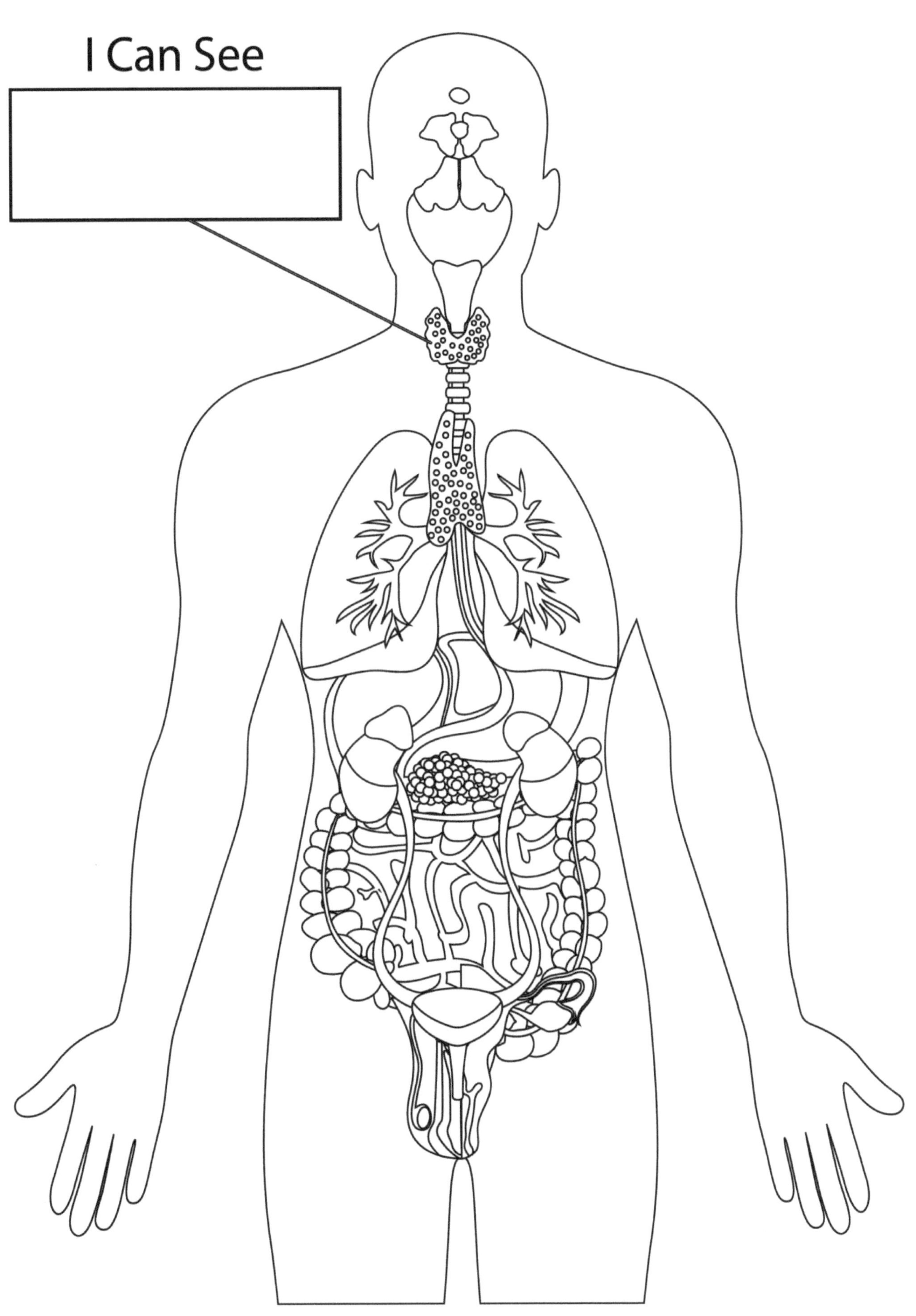

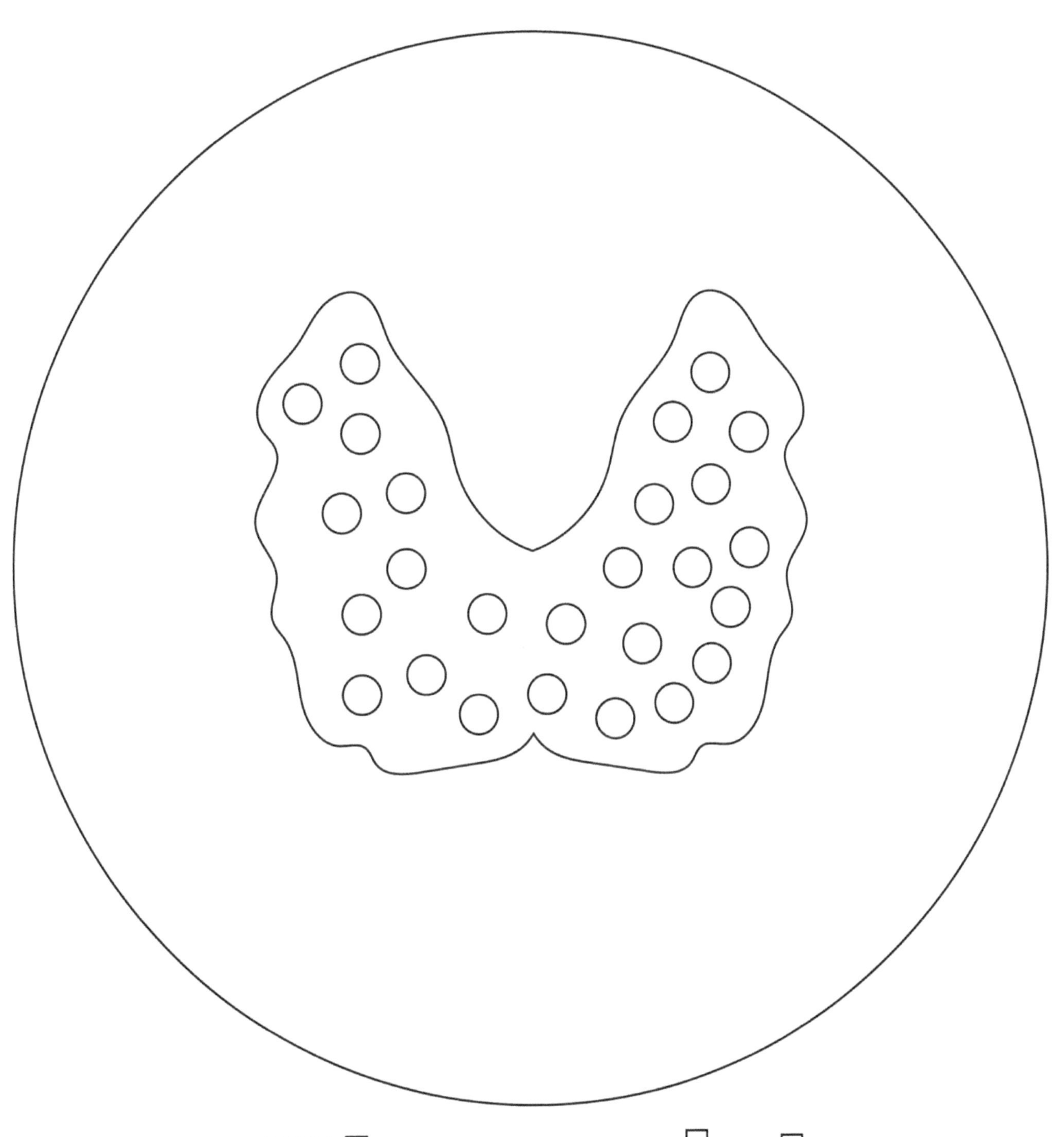

Thyroid

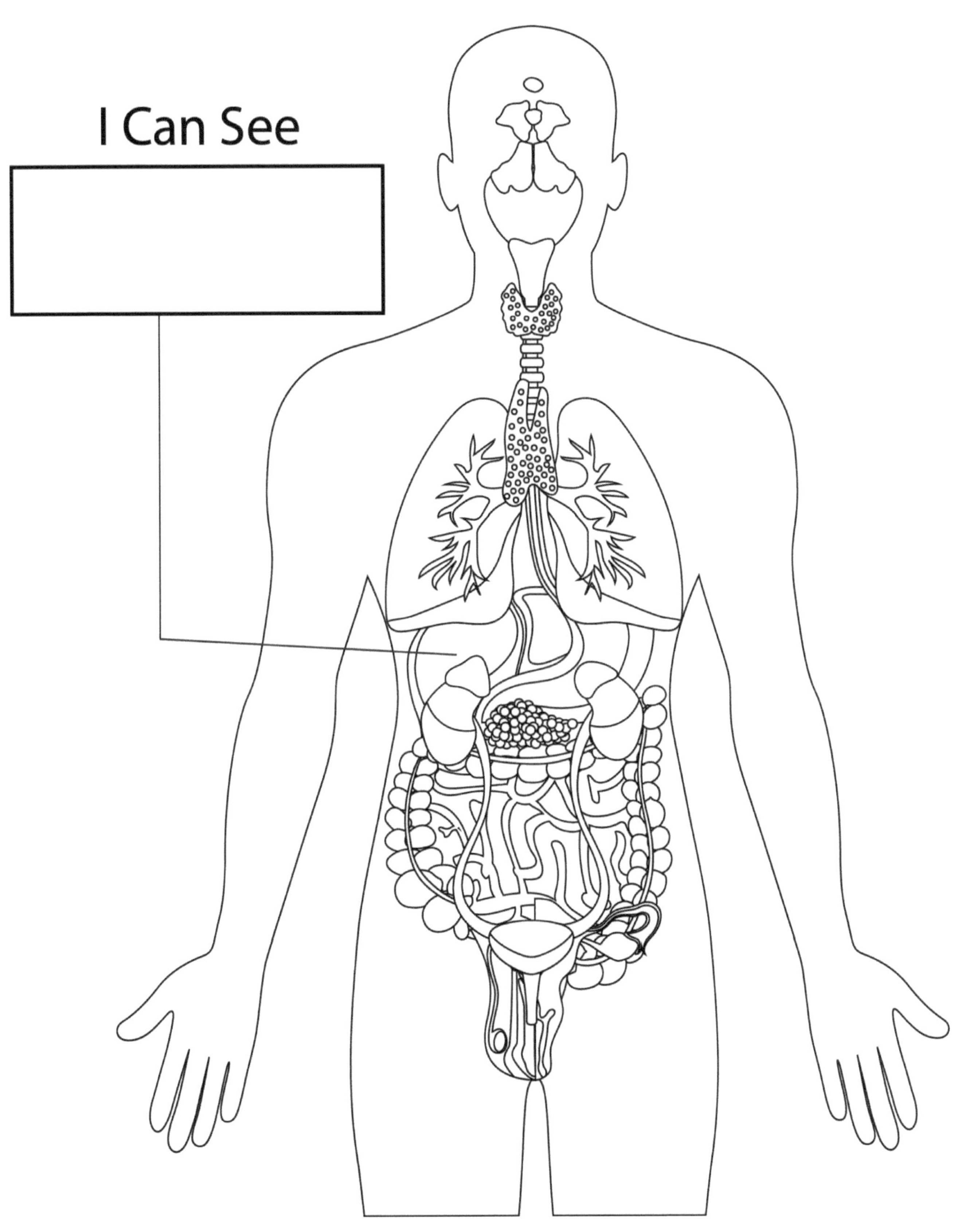

I Can See

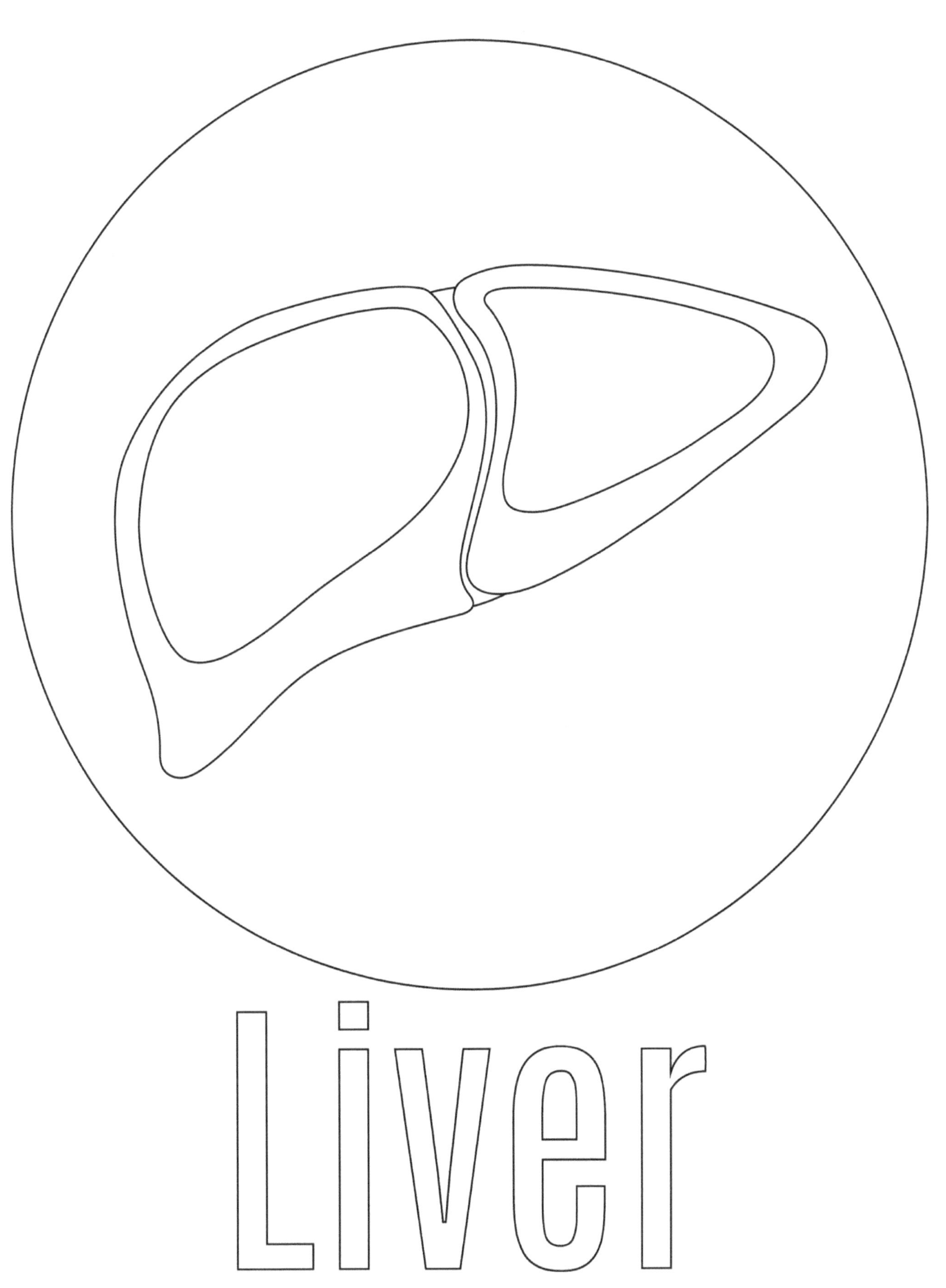

Liver

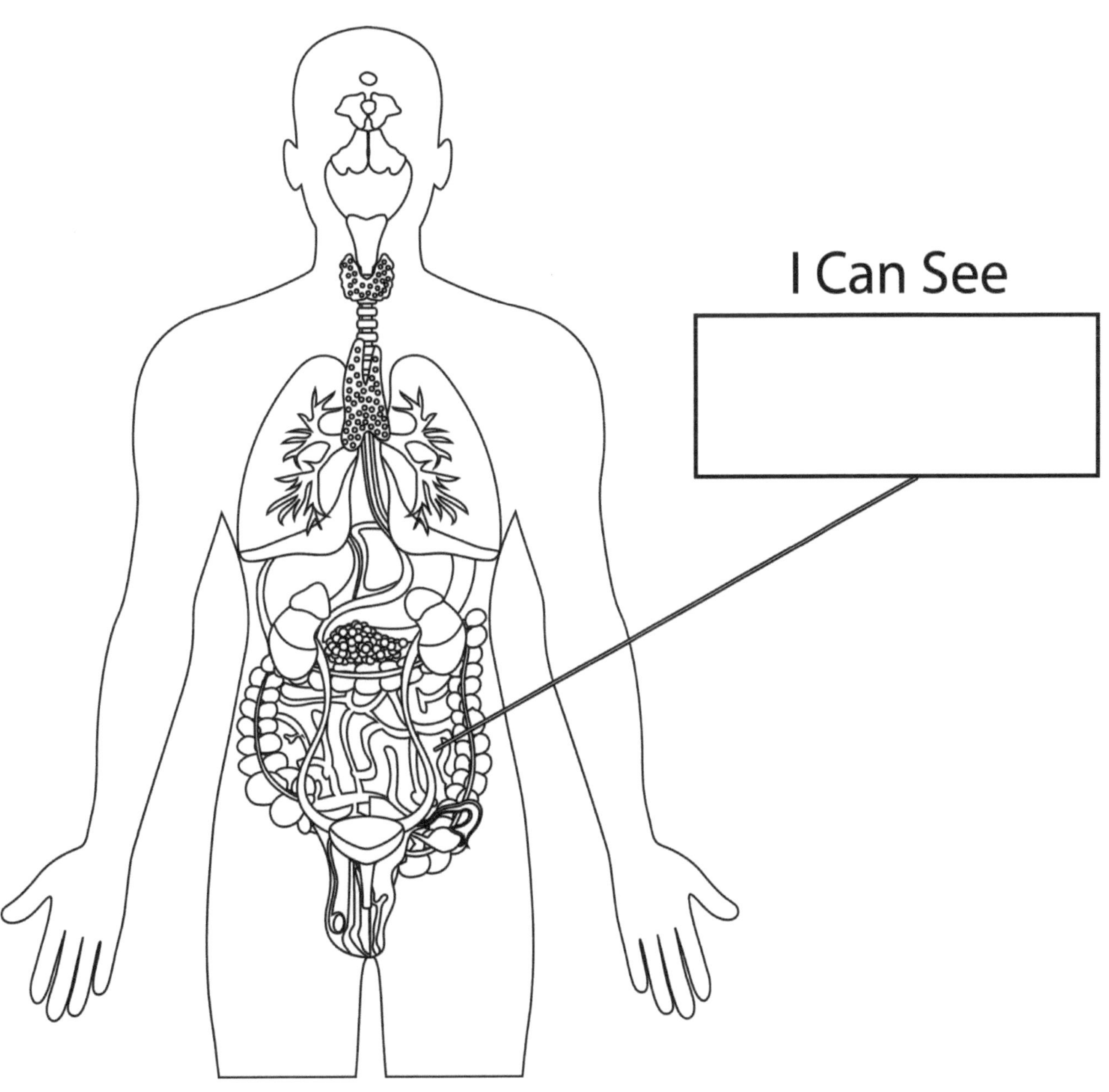

I Can See

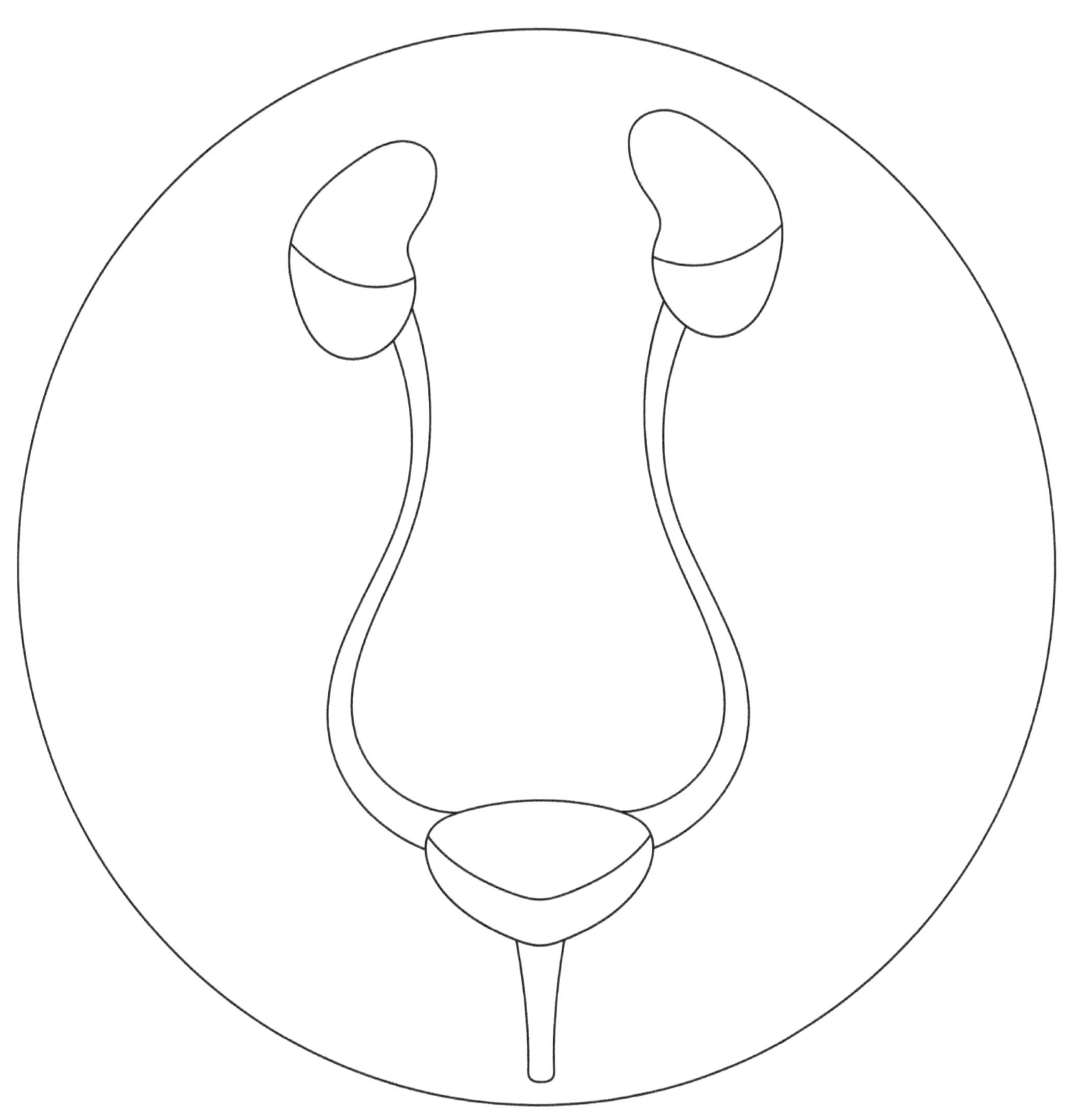

Urinary system

I Can See

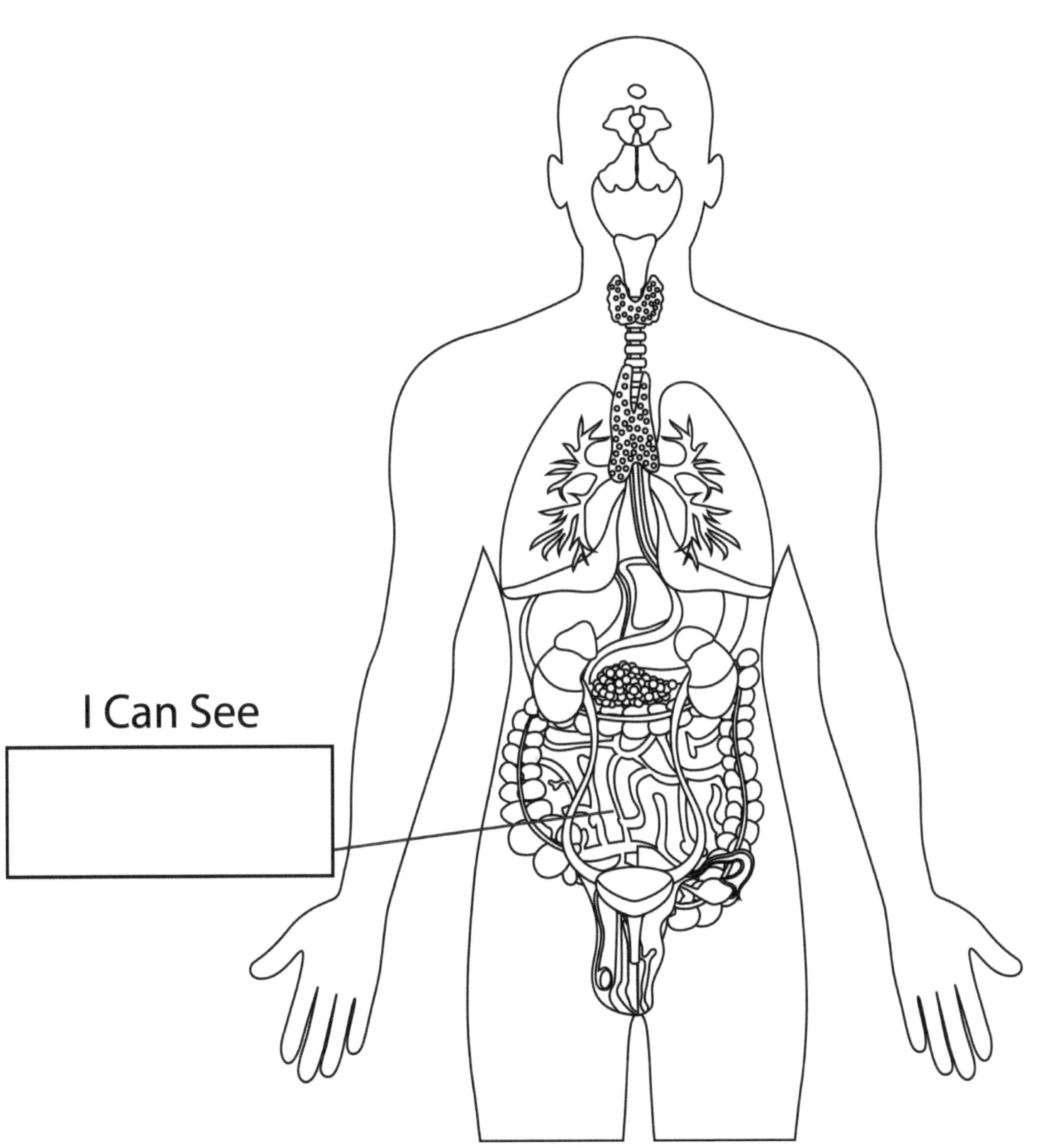

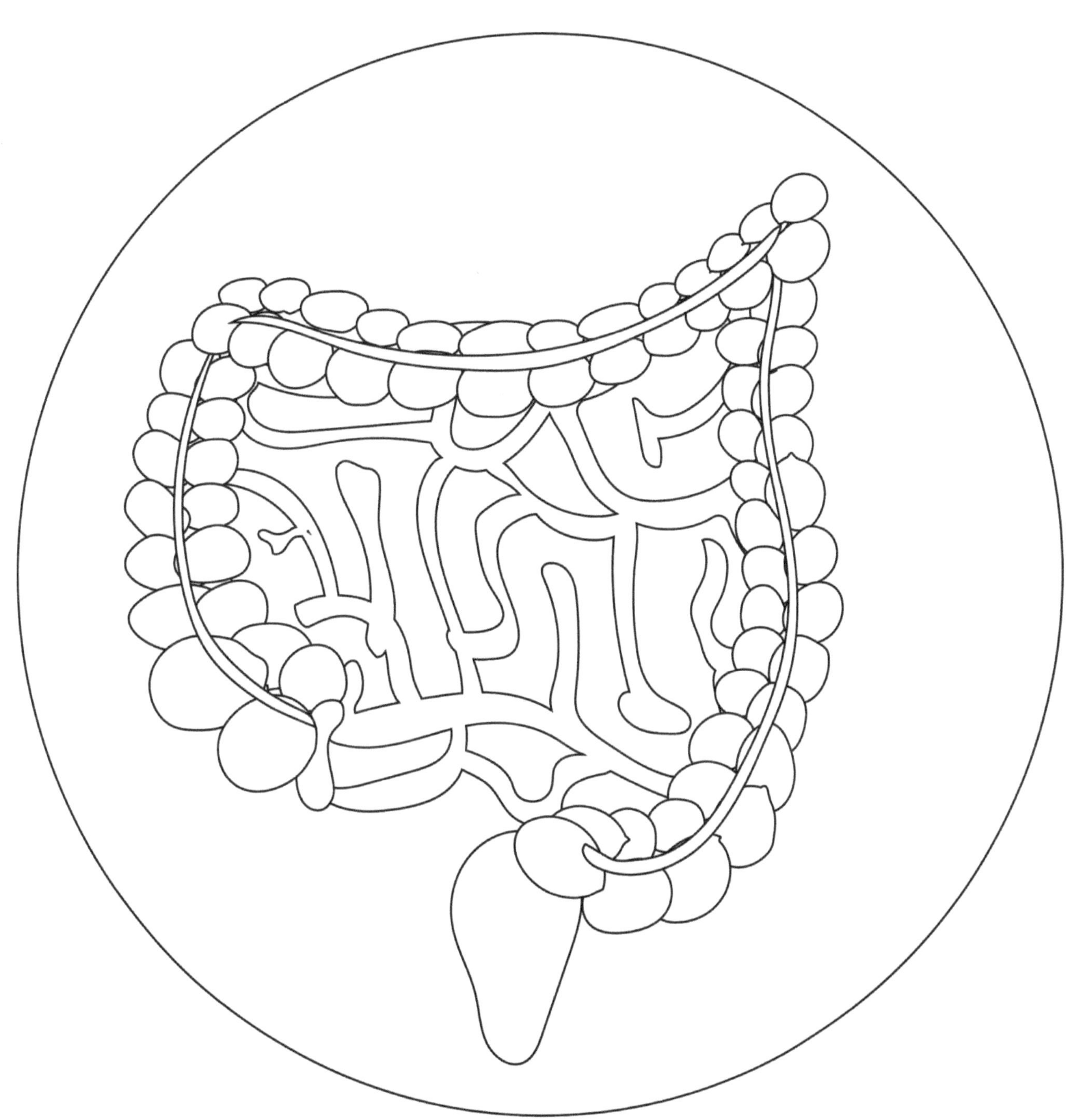

Intestines

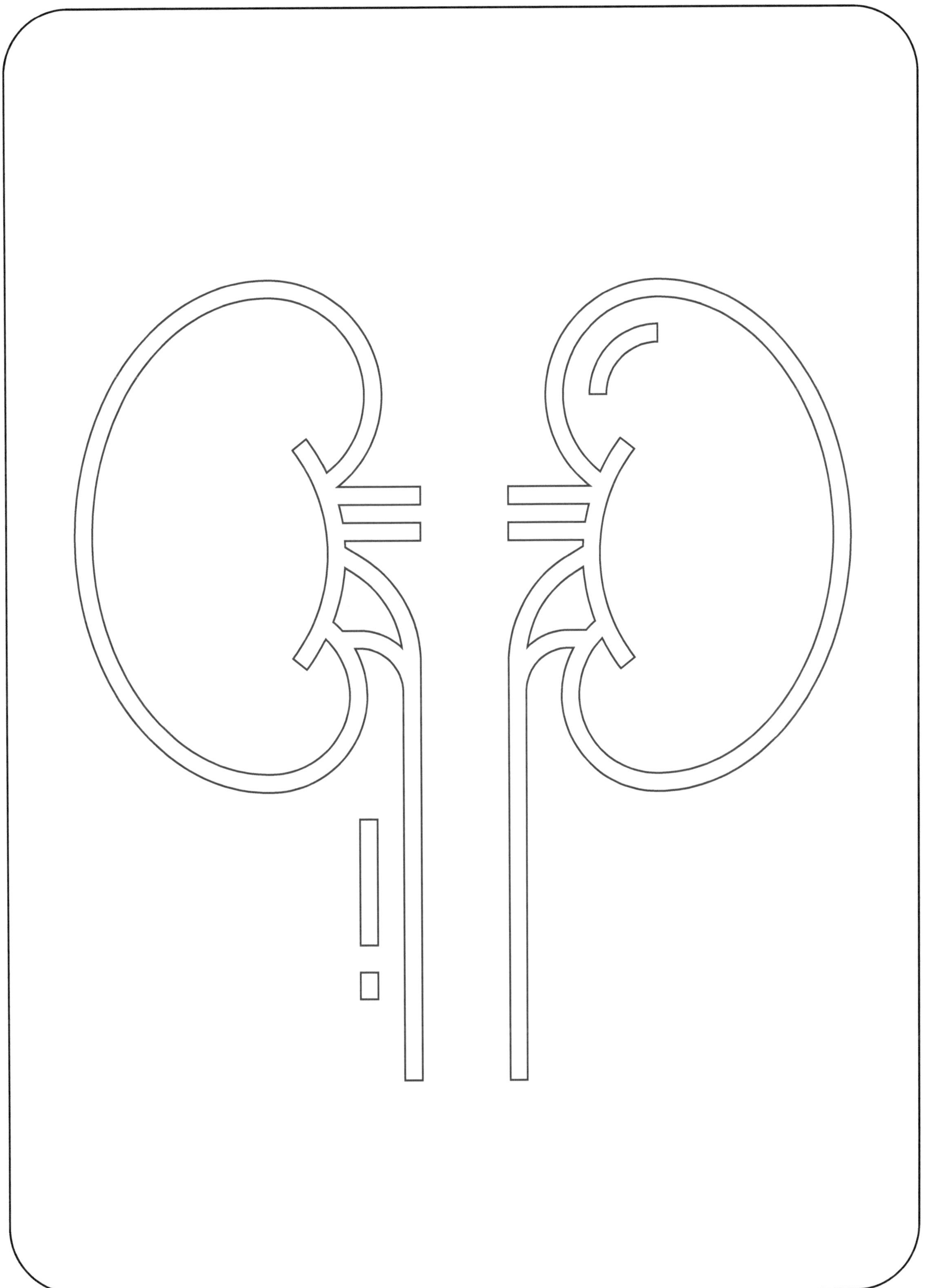

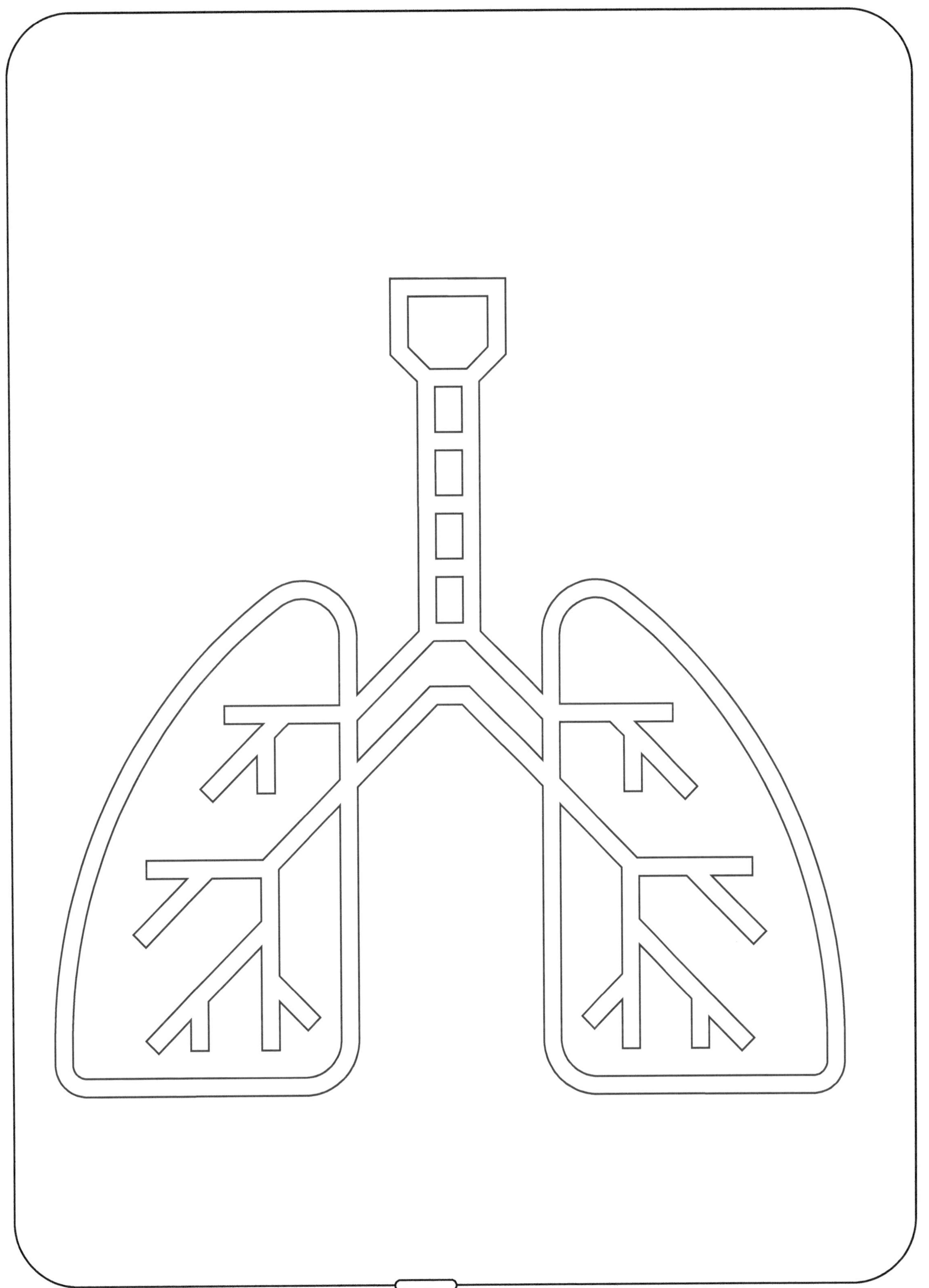

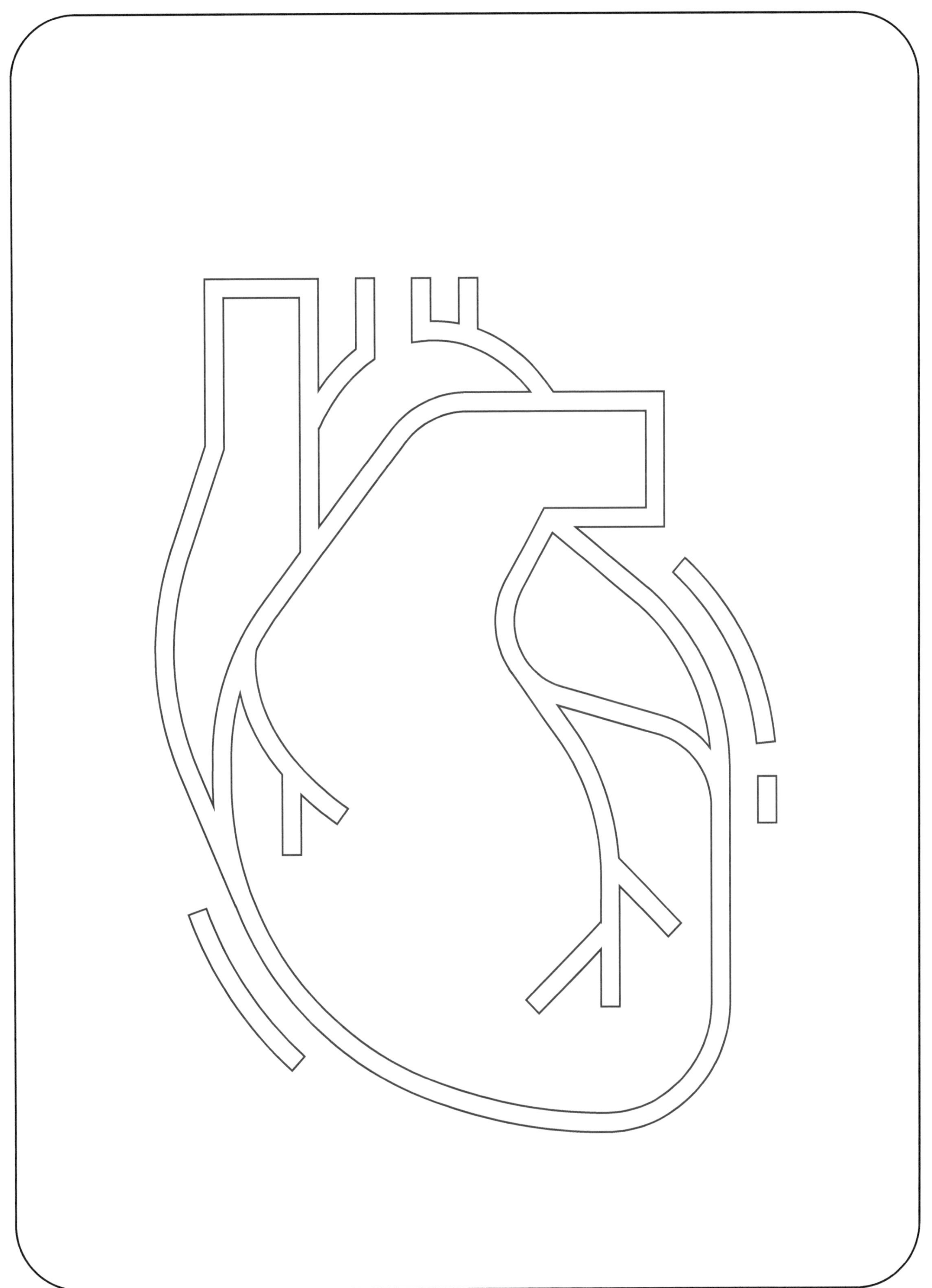

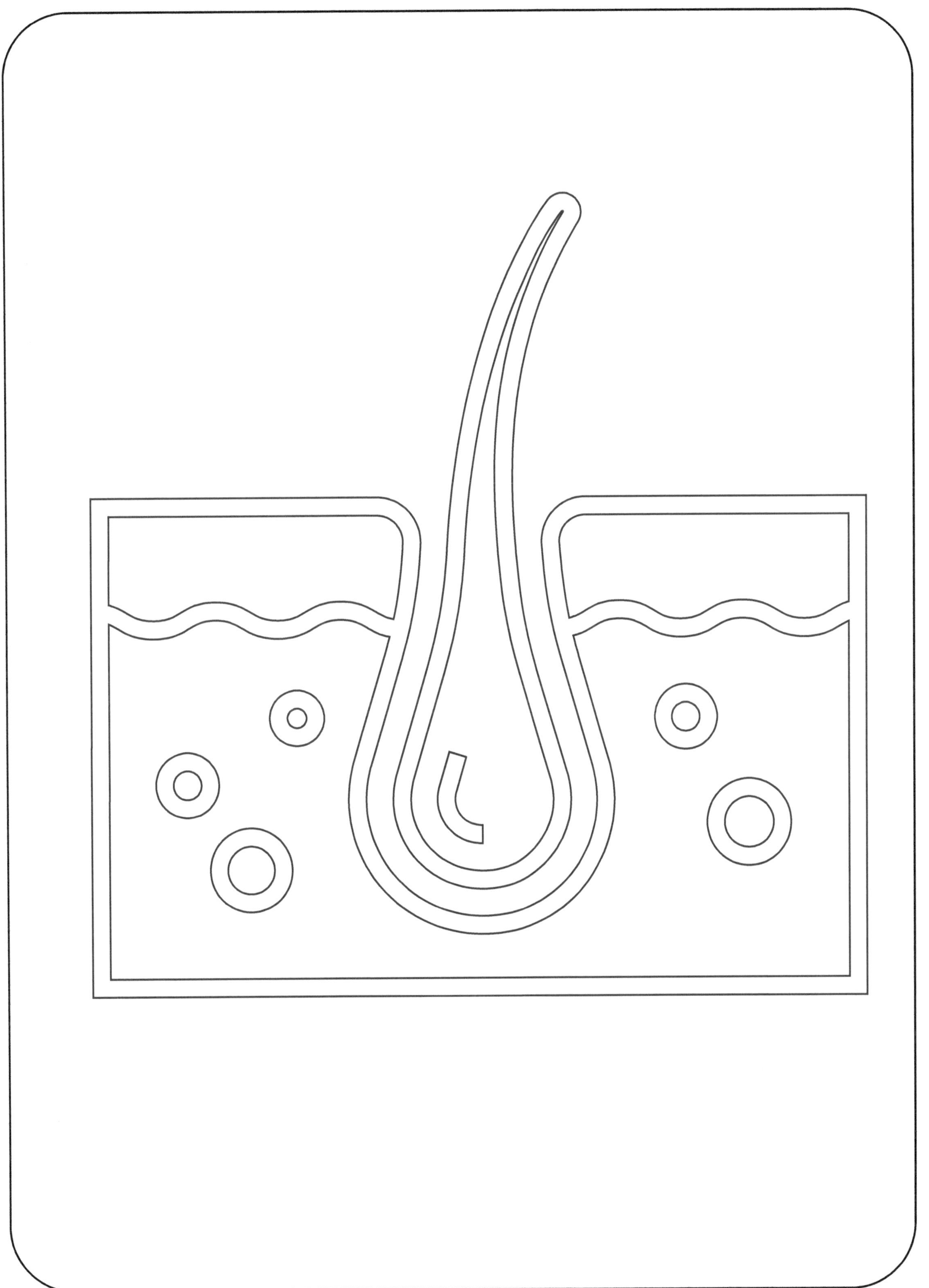

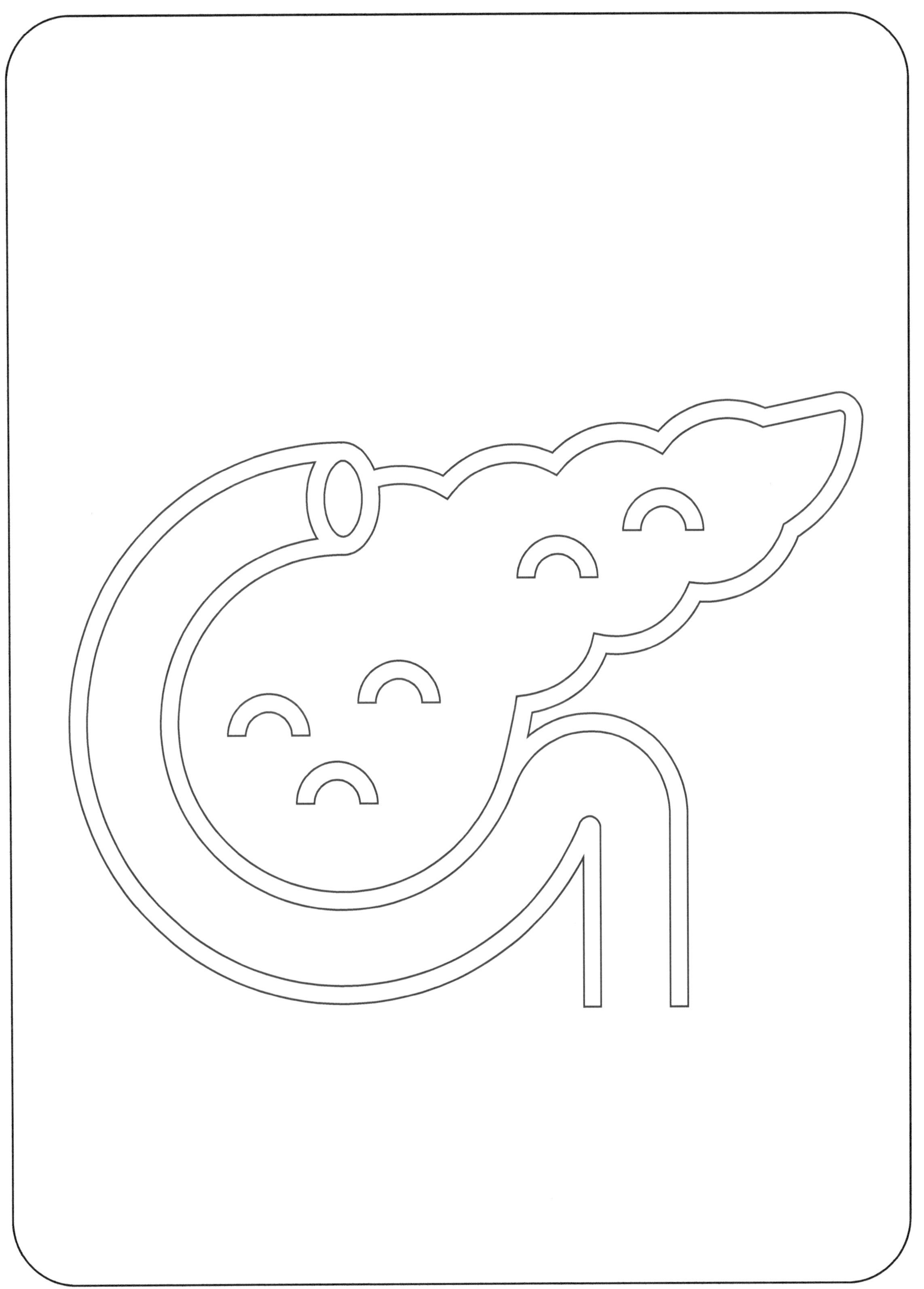

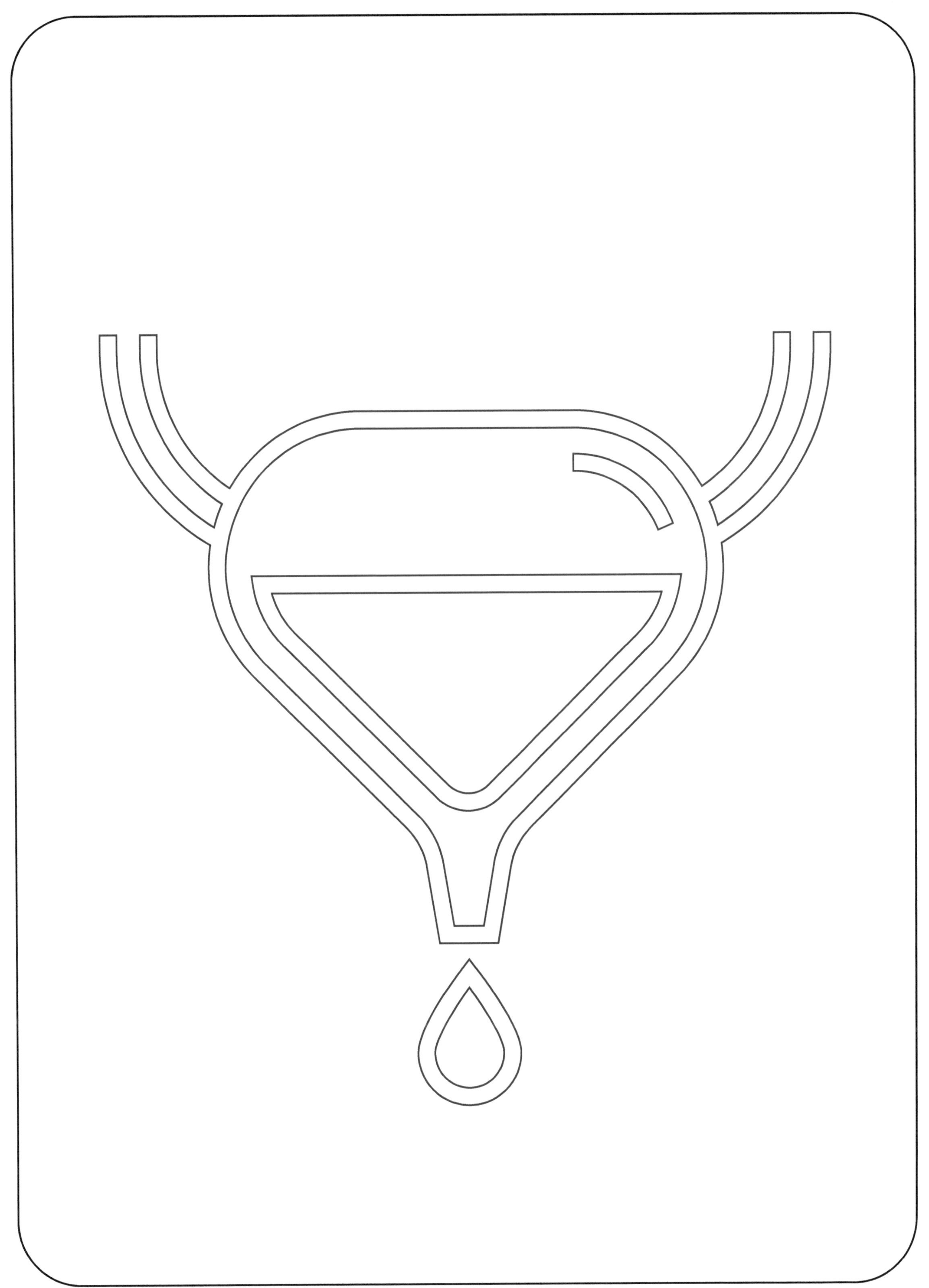

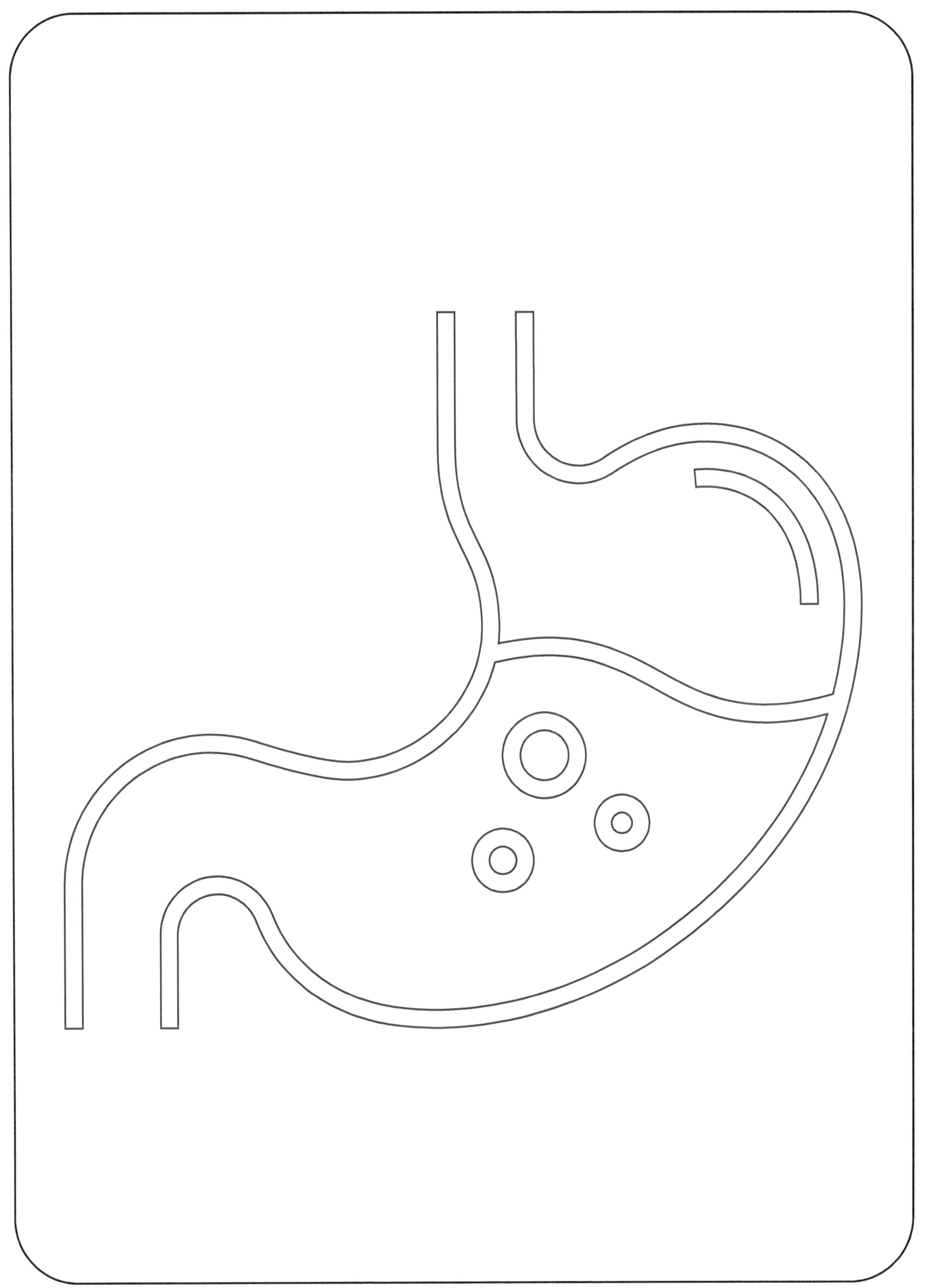

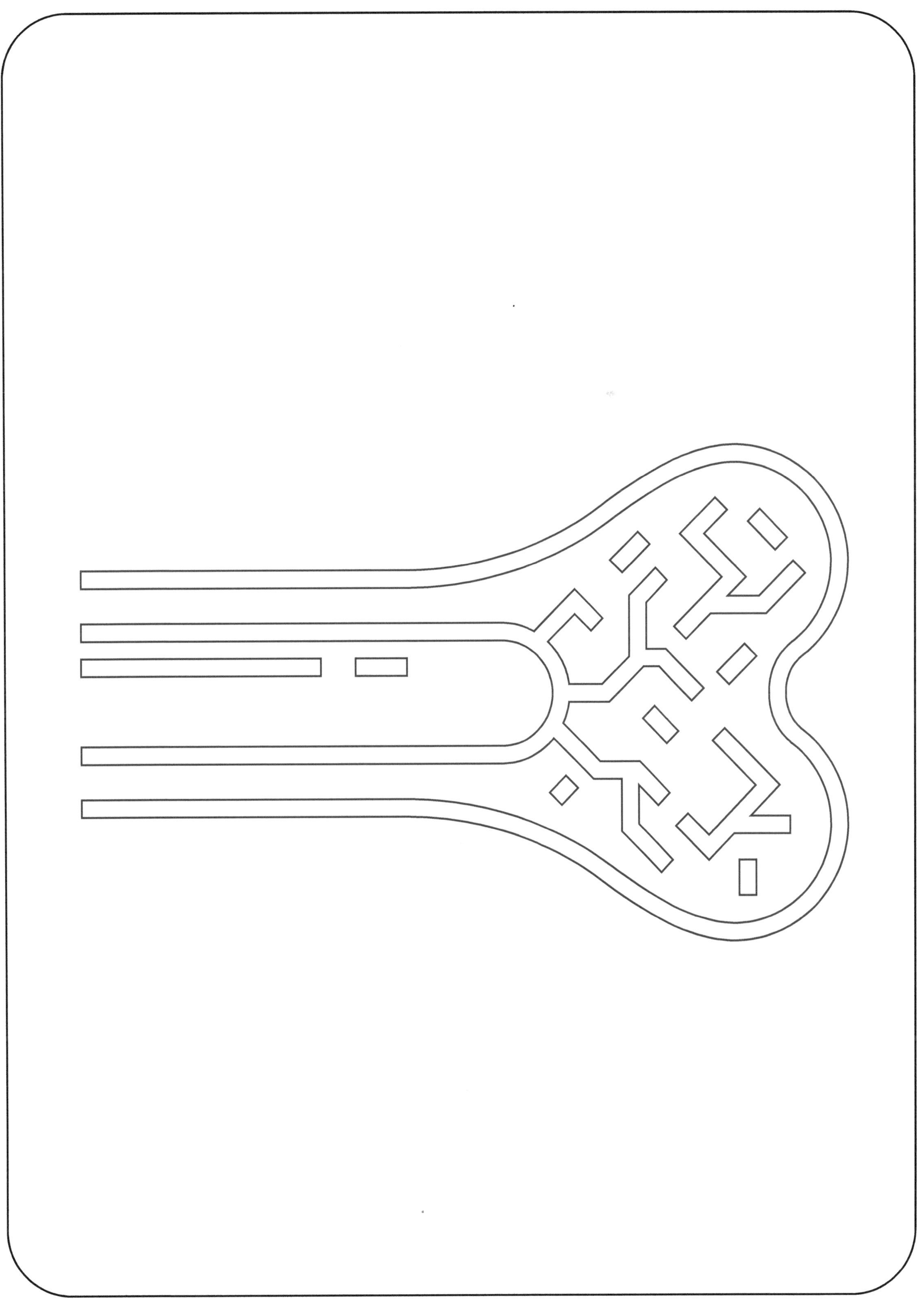

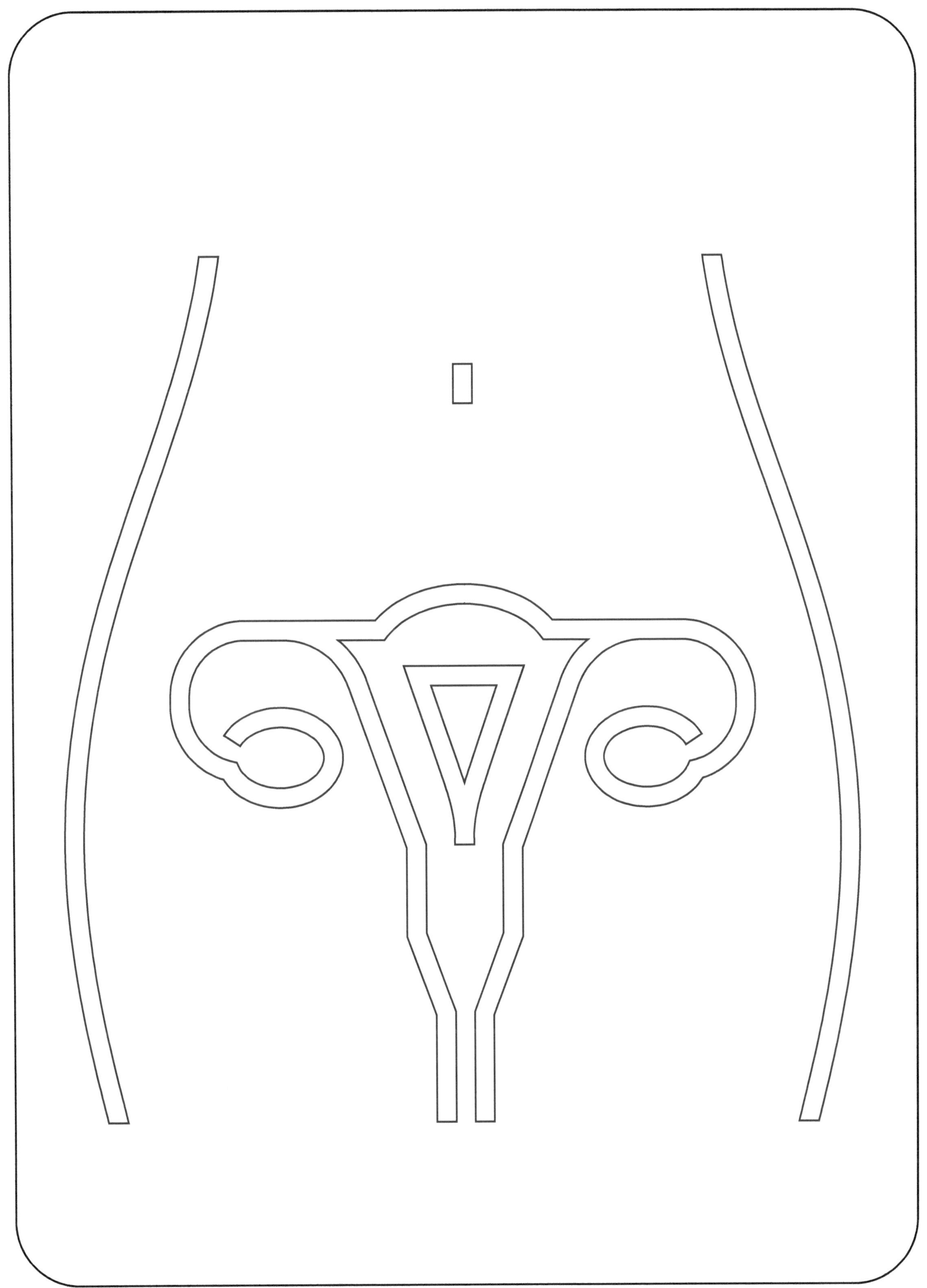

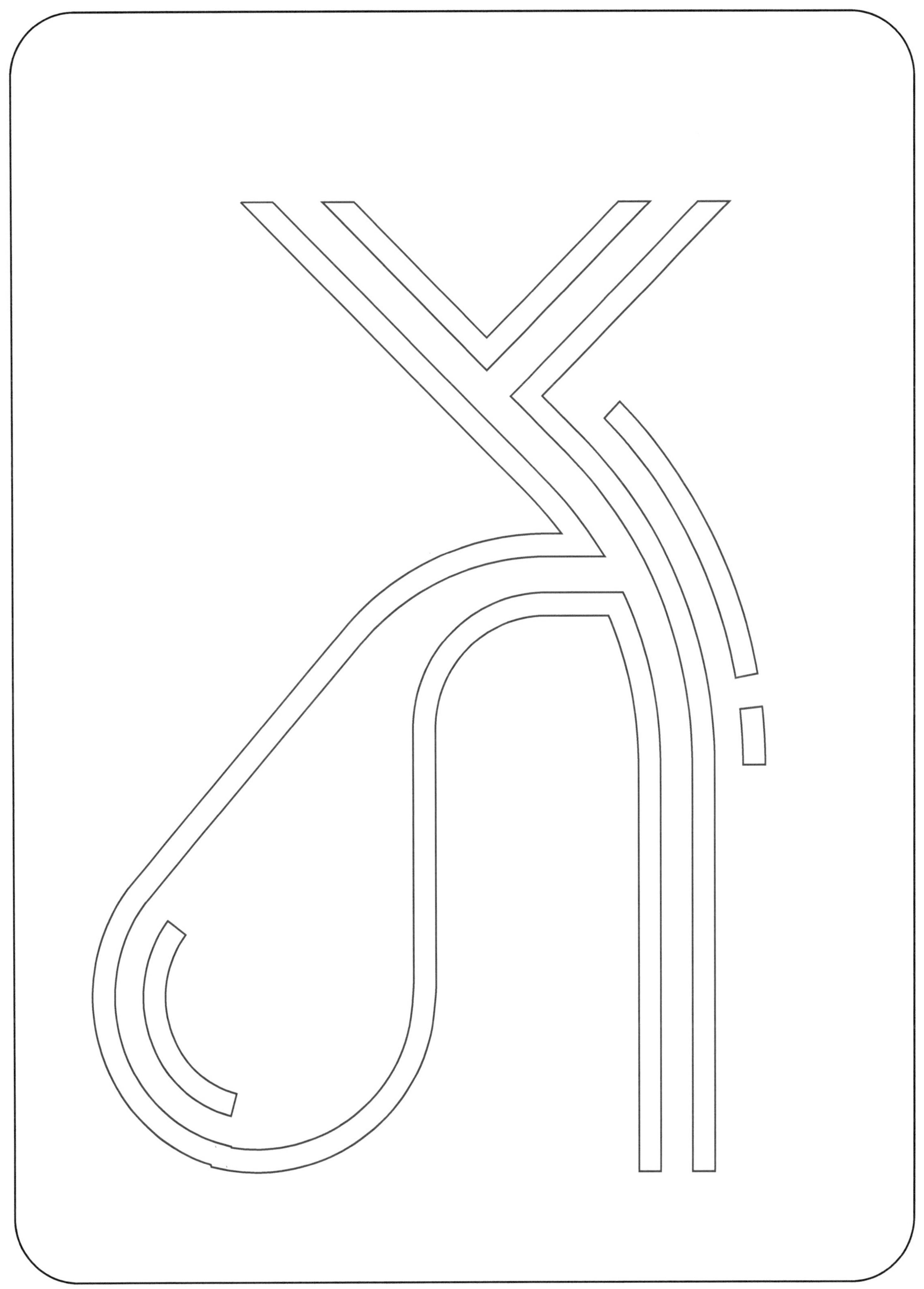

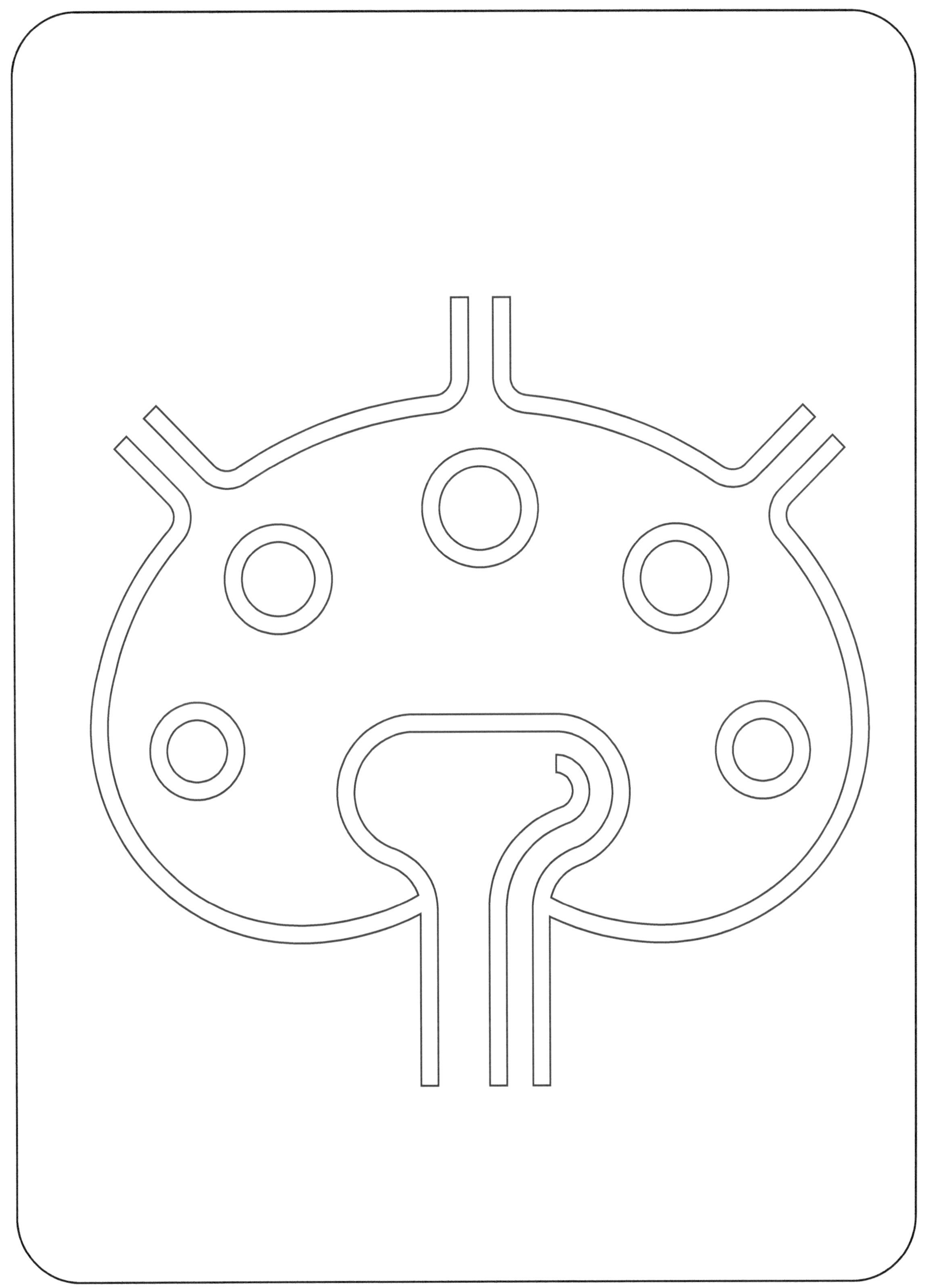

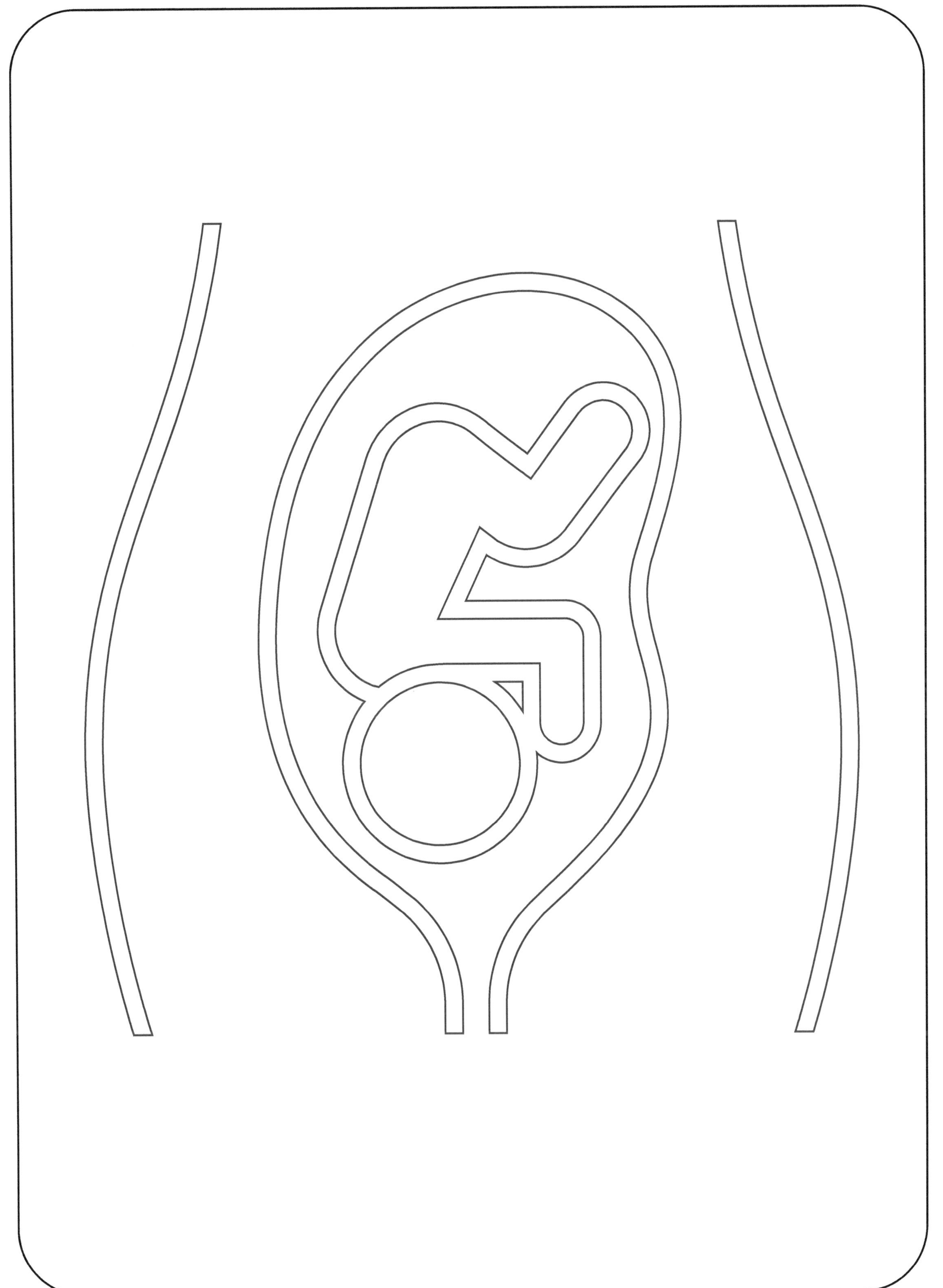

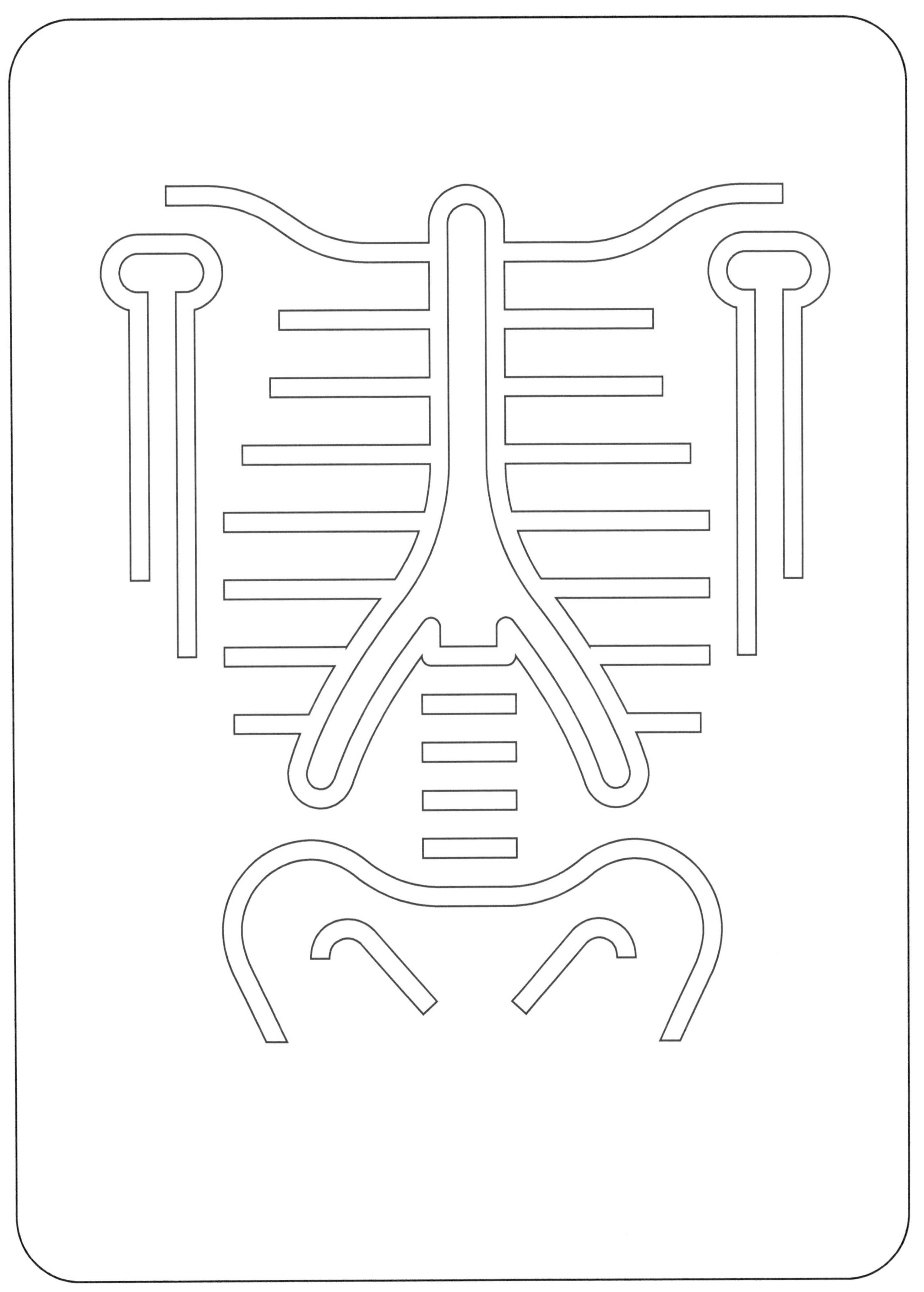

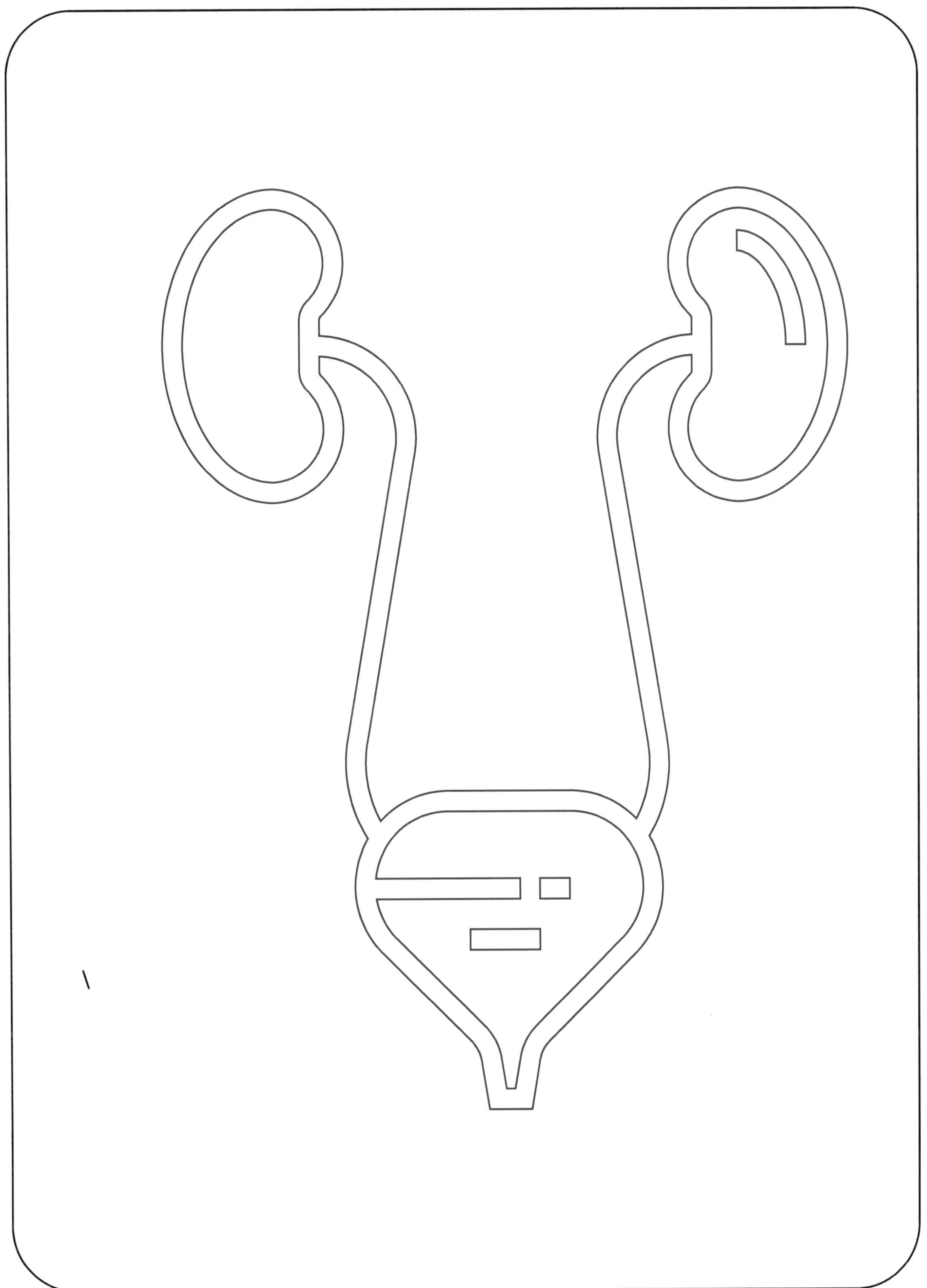

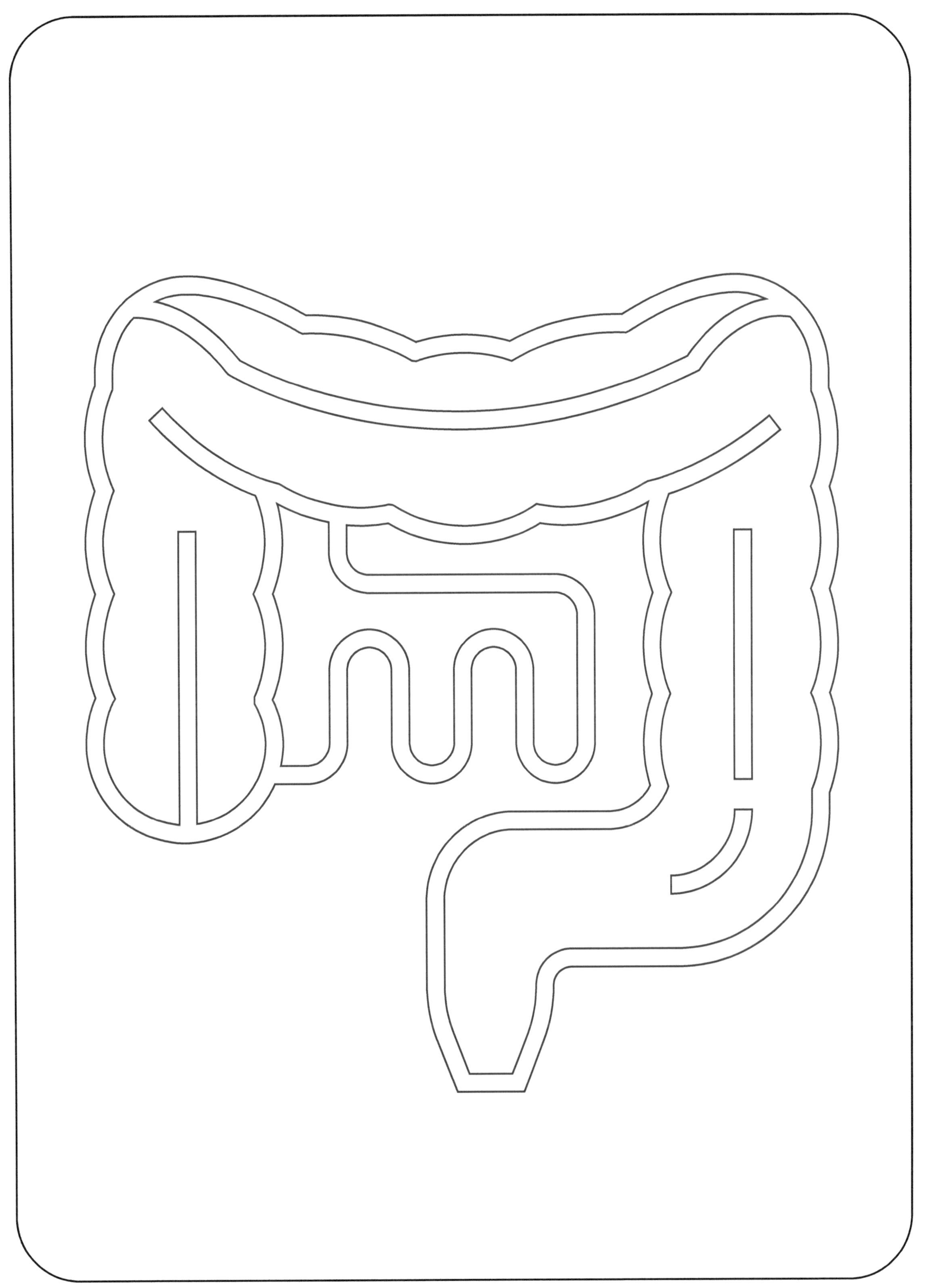

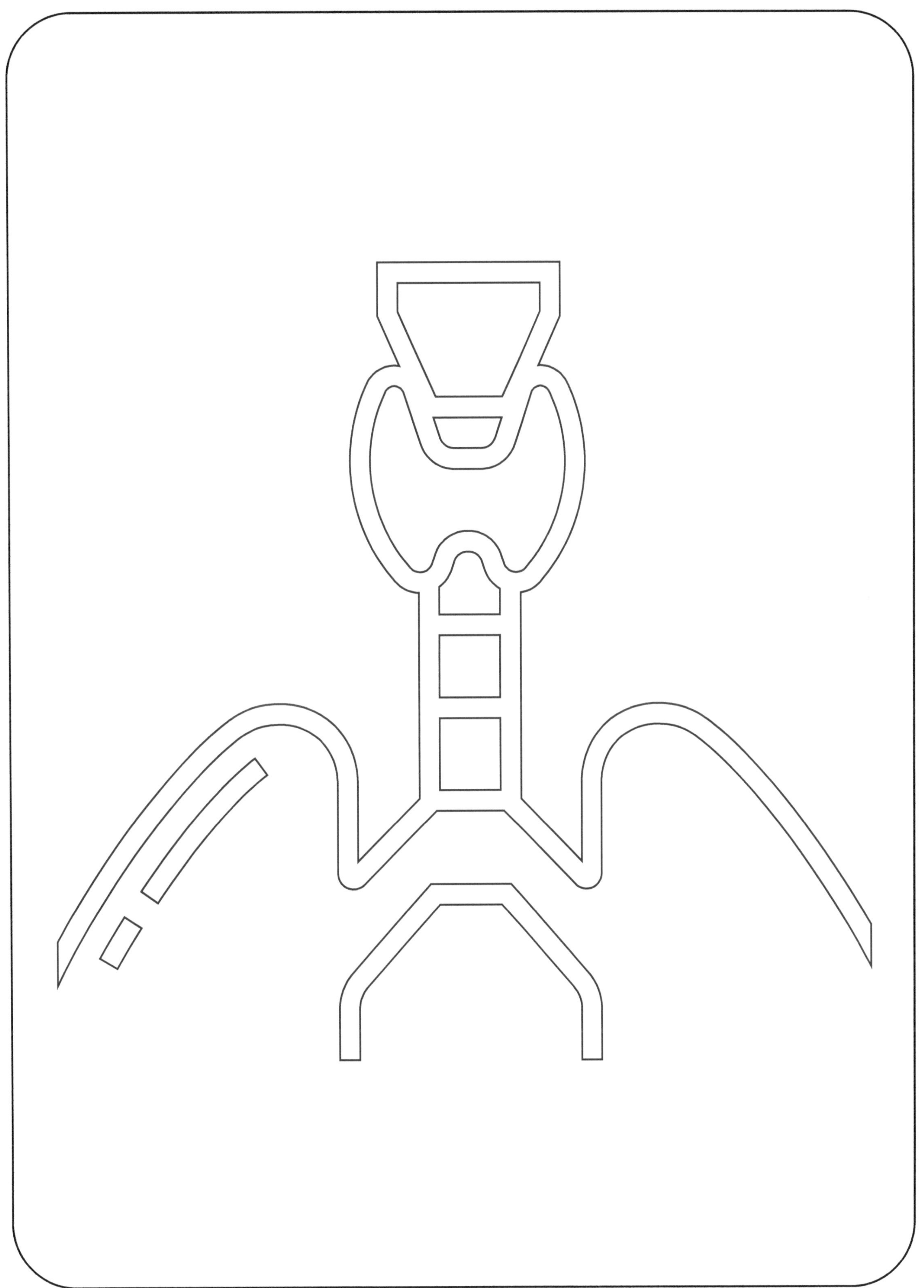

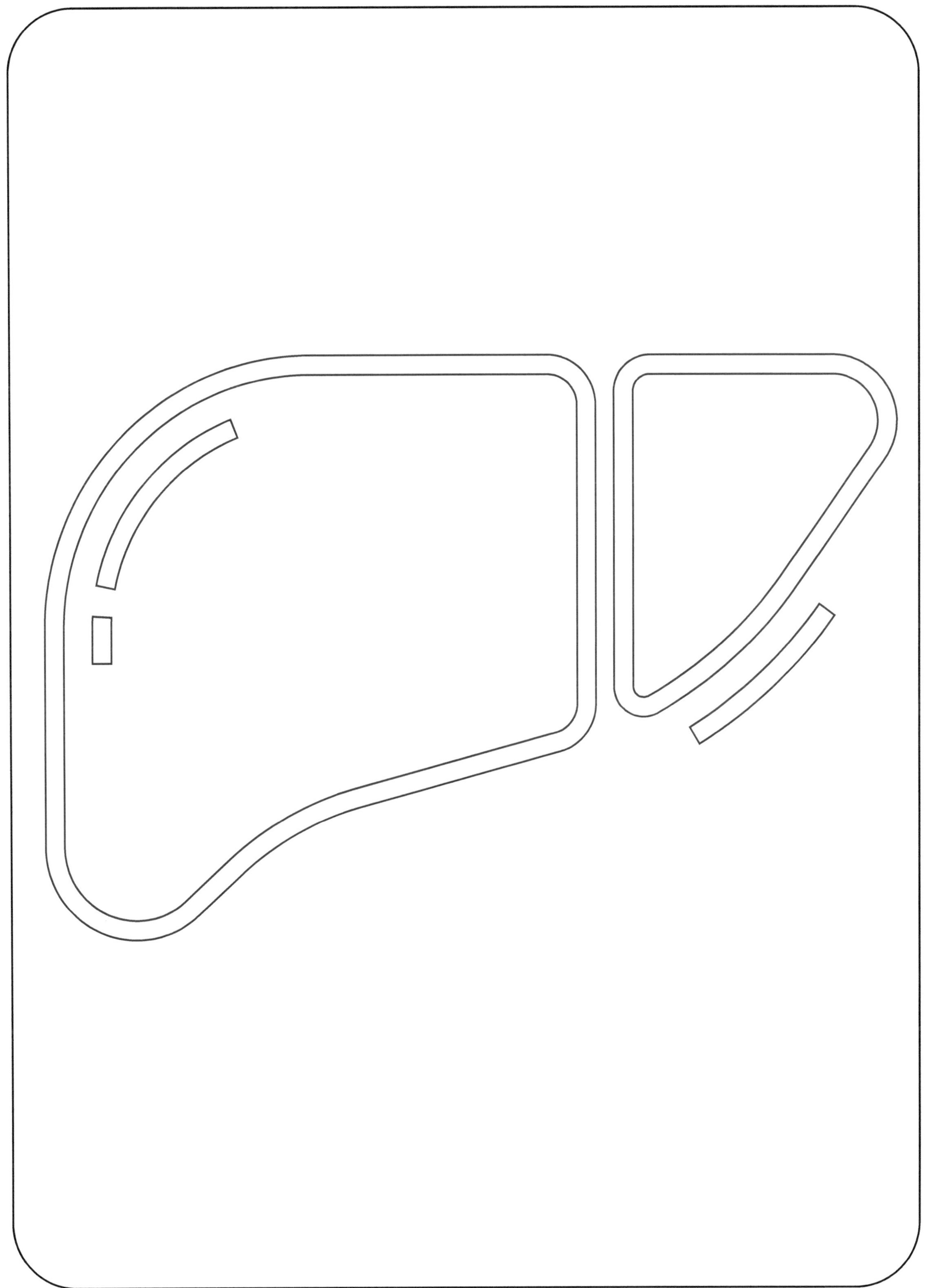

Hey there!!!

We hope you enjoyed our book. As a small family company, your feedback is very important to us. Please let us know how you like our book at:

believepublisher@gmail.com

Without your voice we don't exist!

Please, support us and leave a review!

Thank you!!!

Printed by Libri Plureos GmbH in Hamburg,
Germany